You Can Become the Millionaire Next Door!

Dear Reader:

One hundred years ago, it was virtually impossible for the average person to become a millionaire. Take a look at these lifestyle statistics at the turn of the 20th century:

In 1900, the average wage in this country was 22¢ an hour. The average worker earned between $200 and $400 a year, well below the poverty line at the time. Only 6% of all Americans had graduated from high school. Life expectancy was 47 years old. Only 14% of the homes had a bathtub. There were 8,000 cars in the United States and only 144 miles of paved roads. Until WWI, the average American family spent 80% of their income on the basic necessities of food, shelter, and clothing.

In a word, 100 years ago, there were basically two economic classes: The rich. And the rest. Only one in 10 families was upper class or middle class. Which means that in 1900, 90% of the people in the U.S. would have been classified as poor.

Middle Class Still Living Paycheck to Paycheck

Flash forward 100 years to 2001.

The median family income today is $47,000. There are more cars in this country than people. Most families own at least two TVs. Life expectancy is 75. Today, average people have more disposable income... more leisure time... and more career options than ever before.

Yet most of the nation's 72 million families are still living from paycheck to paycheck. Take away equity in the family home, cars, and furniture, and the average family has zero assets. ZERO! While family income is up, so is family debt and hours spent working.

What's wrong with this picture?

Are You Plugged into the Wrong System?

What's wrong is that too many people have bought into the wrong plan. They're plugged into the wrong system. And they lack a fundamental understanding of how wealth is created and accumulated.

I'm going to made a bold statement that may shock you. But it is absolutely, unequivocally true. Ready?

The simple, unvarnished truth is that today, *becoming a millionaire is a matter of choice, not chance!*

That's right — today, virtually anyone earning a middle class income can become a millionaire. Impossible? Not at all. Actually, it's really quite simple.

If you want to become a millionaire today, all you need to do is follow these three steps:

1) Understand how wealth is created and accumulated
2) Copycat proven systems of wealth creation
3) Be consistent over time

That's it — that's all it takes for average people to accumulate a million dollars in assets: Understanding. Copying. And consistency.

What You Will Learn in This Book

In this book you will learn proven strategies that average people can follow to create true financial freedom for themselves and their families. These strategies are simple to follow and time tested. And they have created millions of millionaires over the last 50 years!

Folks, becoming a millionaire is no longer a matter of good fortune. Or good luck. It's merely a matter of learning and following proven strategies for wealth creation.

In the words of the best-selling book, *The Millionaire Next Door*, "The large majority of millionaires are not the descendants of the Rockefellers or Vanderbilts. *More than 80% are ordinary people* who have accumulated their wealth in one generation."

Think about that — "More than 80% [of millionaires] are ordinary people." This statistic proves what I said earlier — *today, becoming a millionaire is a matter of choice, not chance!*

My goal in writing *The Parable of the Pipeline* is to teach you the strategies the wealthy have used for centuries to create and accumulate wealth. These strategies were once reserved for only the privileged few. Even if you knew these strategies back in 1900, most likely you wouldn't have had the cash or the contacts to take advantage of them. That's not the case today.

Today, by virtue of improved technology... an increase in middle class wages... and an innovative business model I call "e-compounding"... virtually any middle class person with a high school education or above can leverage their money, time, and relationships to create personal and financial freedom.

By following the strategies outlined in this book, you, too, can become the millionaire next door. *Welcome to the neighborhood!*

Yours Truly,

Burke Hedges

THE
PARABLE
OF THE
PIPELINE

The Parable of the Pipeline
*How Anyone Can Build a Pipeline of Ongoing
Residual Income in the New Economy!*

Printed in the United States of America
First Edition January 2001

ISBN: 1-891279-05-x
Published by INTI Publishing
Tampa, FL

Cover design: CherryDesign
Layout: Bayou Graphics

DEDICATION

To everyone who has the wisdom
to become a pipeline builder... and the
willingness to share that wisdom with
others.

ACKNOWLEDGMENT

Discipline, determination, focus, and patience are the words that come to mind when I think of Dr. Steve Price, who was the backbone to the successful completion of this manuscript. Steve, you're extremely talented and relentless in seeing a project through from beginning to end. I appreciate you, and in my eyes, you're truly a "Priceless" partner.

I'm forever grateful to Katherine Glover, President of INTI Publishing. Katherine is a leader extraordinaire, and her input and attention to the details throughout the creation and development of this book were invaluable.

I want to thank Donna Morrison for the outstanding job she did in creating the easy-to-read layout. Donna, you're always a pleasure to work with.

A great big thanks to Liz Cherry and her creative team for their wonderful cover design. Cherry Design hit a home run in conveying the awesome power of residual income.

Any acknowledgment I make would not be complete without thanking everyone at Team INTI: Sandee Lorenzen makes INTI operations run like a Swiss clock; Dee Garrand designed and oversees five of the best websites in the industry; Cindy Hodge not only runs the warehouse efficiently, she does it with a smile on her face and laughter in her voice; Jewel Parago, CFO, is a computer expert and accounting whiz rolled into one (what would we do without you, Jewel?).

Lastly, I want to thank my father for stressing to me when I was a teenager that in life, pipelines are my lifelines. Thanks for your patience and timeless wisdom, Dad.

BOOKS BY BURKE HEDGES

- *Who Stole the American Dream?*

- *You Can't Steal Second with Your Foot on First!*

- *You, Inc.*

- *Copycat Marketing 101*

- *Read and Grow Rich*

- *Dream-Biz.com*

CONTENTS

FROM THE DESK OF BURKE HEDGES

Your Pipelines Are Your Lifelines!

It's been 25 years since my father passed away. But I can still remember our early evening chess games like they were yesterday.

I remember helping my father set up the chess board on the verandah of our beach house overlooking the Pacific Ocean off the coast of Ecuador.

I remember watching the waves breaking against the white sand beach.

I remember the fragrance of hibiscus floating on the saltwater mist.

I remember watching the soft yellow sun sink below the steel-gray horizon.

We'd play chess until dark. My father would talk. I would listen.

"Never take anything for granted," I remember him saying many times as he gazed at the horizon.

From Prince to Pauper in One Day

"Never take anything for granted."

My father was referring to 1959, the year Castro took over Cuba. Prior to the revolution, my father was one of the richest men in Cuba. According to an article in *Time* magazine, my father was worth more than $20 million (which would calculate to at least $200 million in today's dollars). He owned 12 different businesses, including cotton mills, retail stores, a textile mill, a chemical-manufacturing plant, and commercial real estate.

When Castro took over, my parents escaped to Jamaica with just the clothes on their backs. My father's businesses and bank accounts were confiscated for what the communists called "crimes against the people."

My father's only "crime" was being successful... and then taking that success for granted. In hindsight, he should have moved some of his assets out of the country. He took it for granted that Castro would never be able to overthrow the government.

My father was wrong. And it cost him his fortune.

A Premonition of Pipelines

My father did his best to rebuild his dynasty. But a bad economy and a bad heart conspired to prevent his comeback. He wasn't bitter in his final days. He was just disappointed that he had run out of time.

So as we played chess, my father did his best to teach me the key principles that enabled him to amass a small fortune while he was still in his 40s.

My father often lectured me on the importance of owning your own businesses. Ownership meant independence and control. As far as my father was concerned, the more businesses you had, the better.

"Your pipelines are your lifelines," he would say.

I took my father's lessons to heart. I opened my first business when I was only 25 years old. Today I own several fast-growing businesses.

Ironically, one of my companies, Equibore, is a pipeline business — *literally*! Equibore installs the underground conduit that "Old Economy" utility companies use to house their gas and water pipelines. "New Economy" telecom companies use the conduit for their fiber optic cables, the pipelines of the future.

My Rich Dad, His Rich Dad

My father was a big believer in diversification. That's why most of his 12 different businesses were in different industries.

"If you've only got one pipeline, then you've only got one lifeline," he'd say as he captured one of my chess pieces. "The more pipelines you've got, the better."

A few months ago I came across an audio tape by Robert Kiyosaki titled, *What My Rich Dad Taught Me About Investing*. Kiyosaki tells a brief story about two young men who were hired to deliver water from a lake to their village a mile away. One of the young men used buckets to carry the water. The other young man built a pipeline. Over the long run, the young man who built the pipeline fared far better than the bucket carrier.

Kiyosaki's audio reminded me of the lessons my father taught me 25 years ago. That evening I went home and jotted down 10 pages of notes for a new book explaining the parallel between pipelines and lifelines and urging readers to diversify their income streams by building both short-term and long-term pipelines.

I titled the book, *The Parable of the Pipeline*.

Three months later I handed my publisher the manuscript to the book you're holding in your hands.

Building Your Own Pipelines

Over the years I've taken my father's advice and built several profitable pipelines. I don't own 12 businesses like he did. And I'm not worth $20 million yet.

But I'm working on it.

Pipelines are designed to take the worry out of people's lives by putting profits into their pockets. But most of all, pipelines are designed to give people personal and financial freedom and lifelong security.

In short, pipelines are lifelines.

My father had his lifelines taken from him

by a dictator. And he never recovered. People in this country are blessed — we'll never have our lifelines taken from us by a dictator. Only we can take the lifelines from ourselves.

How?

By not taking the initiative to build them!

Take a lesson from my father — don't take it for granted that tomorrow will be just the same as today. Because it won't!

The only security is the security of a pipeline.

I urge you to start building your pipelines today... so that you'll have your lifelines tomorrow!

INTRODUCTION

INTRODUCTION

The Parable of the Pipeline

1801, valley in central Italy

ONCE UPON A TIME LONG, LONG AGO, two ambitious young cousins named Pablo and Bruno lived side by side in a small Italian village.

The young men were best buddies.

And big dreamers.

They would talk endlessly about how some day, some way, they would become the richest men in the village. They were both bright and hard working. All they needed was an opportunity.

One day that opportunity arrived. The village decided to hire two men to carry water from a nearby river to a cistern in the town square. The job went to Pablo and Bruno.

Each man grabbed two buckets and headed to the river. By the end of the day, they had filled the town cistern to the brim. The village elder paid them one penny for each bucket of water.

"This is our dream come true!" shouted Bruno. *"I can't believe our good fortune."*

But Pablo wasn't so sure.

His back ached and his hands were blistered from carrying the heavy buckets. He dreaded getting up and going to work the next morning. He vowed to think of a better way of getting the water from the river to the village.

Pablo, the Pipeline Man

"Bruno, I have a plan," Pablo said the next morning as they grabbed their buckets and headed for the river. "Instead of lugging buckets back and forth for pennies a day, let's build a pipeline from the river to the village."

Bruno stopped dead in his tracks.

"A pipeline! Whoever heard of such a thing?" Bruno shouted. "We've got a great job, Pablo. I can carry 100 buckets a day. At a penny a bucket, that's a dollar a day! I'm rich! By the end of the week, I can buy a new pair of shoes. By the end of the month, a cow. By the end of six months, I can build a new hut. We have the best job in town. We have weekends off and two weeks' paid vacation every year. We're set for life! Get out of here with your pipeline."

But Pablo was not easily discouraged. He patiently explained the pipeline plan to his best friend. Pablo would work part of the day carrying buckets and then part of the day and weekends building his pipeline. He knew it would be hard work digging a ditch in the rocky soil. Because he was paid by the bucket, he knew his income would drop at first. He also knew it would take a year, possibly two, before his pipeline would start to pay big dividends. But Pablo believed in his dream, and he went to work.

Pipeline in Progress

Bruno and the rest of the villagers began mocking Pablo, calling him "Pablo the Pipeline Man." Bruno, who was earning almost twice as much money as Pablo, flaunted his new purchases. He bought a donkey outfitted with a new leather saddle, which he kept parked outside his new two-story hut. He bought flashy clothes and fancy meals at the inn. The villagers called him Mr. Bruno, and they cheered when he bought rounds at the tavern and laughed loudly at his jokes.

Small Actions Equal Big Results

While Bruno lay in his hammock on evenings and weekends, Pablo kept digging his pipeline. The first few months Pablo didn't have much to show for his efforts. The work was hard —

even harder than Bruno's because Pablo was working evenings and weekends, too.

But Pablo kept reminding himself that tomorrow's dreams are built on today's sacrifices. Day by day he dug, an inch at a time.

"Inch by inch it's a cinch," he chanted to himself as he swung his pickax into the rocky soil. Inches turned into one foot... then 10 feet... then 20... 100....

"Short-term pain equals long-term gain," he reminded himself as he stumbled into his humble hut exhausted from another day's work. He measured his success by setting and meeting his daily goals, knowing that, over time, the results would far exceed his efforts.

"Keep your eyes on the prize," he repeated over and over as he drifted off to sleep accompanied by the sounds of laughter from the village tavern.

"Keep your eyes on the prize...."

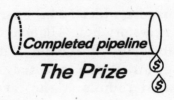

The Prize

The Tables Are Turned

Days turned into months. One day Pablo realized his pipeline was halfway finished, which meant he only had to walk half as far to fill up his buckets! Pablo used the extra time to work on his pipeline. The completion date was advancing faster and faster.

During his rest breaks, Pablo watched his old friend Bruno lug buckets. Bruno's shoulders were more stooped than ever. He was hunched in pain, his steps slowed by the daily grind. Bruno was angry and sullen, resenting the fact that he was doomed to carry buckets, day in and day out, for the rest of his life.

He began spending less time in his hammock and more time in the tavern. When the tavern's patrons saw Bruno coming, they'd whisper, "Here comes Bruno the Bucket Man," and they'd giggle when the town drunk mimicked Bruno's stooped posture and shuffling gait. Bruno didn't buy rounds or tell jokes anymore, preferring to sit alone in a dark corner surrounded by empty bottles.

Finally, Pablo's big day arrived — the pipeline was complete! The villagers crowded around as the water gushed from the pipeline into the village cistern! Now that the village had a steady supply of fresh water, people from the surrounding countryside moved into the village, and it grew and prospered.

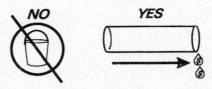

Once the pipeline was complete, Pablo didn't have to carry buckets anymore. The water flowed whether he worked or not. It flowed while he ate. It flowed while he slept. It flowed on the weekends while he played. The more the water flowed into the village, the more the money flowed into Pablo's pockets!

Pablo the Pipeline Man became known as Pablo the Miracle Maker. Politicians lauded him for his vision and begged him to run for mayor. But Pablo understood that what he had accomplished wasn't a miracle. It was merely the first stage of a big, big dream. You see, Pablo had plans that reached far beyond his village.

Pablo planned to build pipelines all over the world!

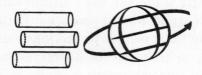

Recruiting His Friend to Help

The pipeline drove Bruno the Bucket Man out of business, and it pained Pablo to see his old friend begging for free drinks in the tavern. So, Pablo arranged a meeting with Bruno.

"Bruno, I've come here to ask you for your help."

Bruno straightened his stooped shoulders, and his dark eyes narrowed to a squint. "Don't mock me," Bruno hissed.

"I haven't come here to gloat," said Pablo. "I've come here to offer you a great business opportunity. It took me more than two years before my first pipeline was complete. But I've learned a lot during those two years! I know what tools to use. Where to dig. How to lay the pipe. I kept notes as I went along, and I've developed a system that will allow me to build another pipeline... and then another... and another.

"I could build a pipeline a year by myself. But that would not be the best use of my time. What I plan to do is to teach you and others how to build a pipeline... and then have you teach others... and have each of them teach others... until there is a pipeline to every village in the region... then a pipeline to every village in the country... and eventually, a pipeline to every village in the world!

"Just think," Pablo continued, "we could make a small percentage of every gallon of water that goes through those pipelines. The more water that flows through the pipelines, the more money that will flow into our pockets. *The pipeline I built isn't the end of a dream. It's only the beginning!*"

Bruno finally saw the Big Picture. He smiled and extended his callused hand to his old friend. They shook hands... and then hugged like long-lost friends.

Pipeline Dreams in a Bucket-Carrying World

Years passed. Pablo and Bruno had long since retired. Their worldwide pipeline business was still pumping millions of dollars a year into their bank accounts. Sometimes on their trips through the countryside, Pablo and Bruno would pass young men carrying water buckets.

The childhood friends would pull over and tell the young men their story and offer to help them build their own pipeline. A few would listen and jump at the opportunity to start a pipeline business. But sadly, most bucket carriers would hastily dismiss the notion of a pipeline. Pablo and Bruno heard the same excuses over and over.

"I don't have the time."

"My friend told me he knew a friend of a friend who tried to build a pipeline and failed."

"Only the ones who get in early make money on pipelines."

"I've carried buckets all my life. I'll stick with what I know."

"I know some people who lost money in a pipeline scam. Not me."

It made Pablo and Bruno sad that so many people lacked vision.

But both men resigned themselves to the fact that they lived in a bucket-carrying world... and that only a small percentage of people dared to dream pipeline dreams.

PART I

We Live in a
Bucket-Carrying World

Who Are You — a Bucket Carrier? Or a Pipeline Builder?

> "Bruno, I have a plan," Pablo said the next morning as they grabbed their buckets and headed for the river. "Instead of lugging buckets back and forth for pennies a day, let's build a pipeline from the river to the village."
>
> Bruno stopped dead in his tracks.
>
> "*A Pipeline! Whoever heard of such a thing?!!*" Bruno shouted.
>
> — from *The Parable of the Pipeline*

Who are you?... A bucket carrier? Or a pipeline builder?

Do you get paid only when you show up and do the work, like Bruno the Bucket Carrier?

Or do you do the work once and then get paid over and over again, like Pablo the Pipeline Builder?

If you're like most people, you're working the bucket-carrying plan. I call it the "Time-for-Money Trap." You know the drill:

One hour's work equals one hour's pay.
One month's work equals one month's pay.
One year's work equals one year's pay.
Sound familiar?

 = Time-for-Money Trap

The problem with bucket carrying is that the money stops when the bucket carrying stops. Which means the concept of a "secure job" or a "dream job" is an illusion. The inherent danger of carrying buckets is that the income is temporary instead of ongoing.

If Bruno woke up one morning with a stiff back and couldn't get out of bed, how much money would he earn that day? *Zero!*

No work, no money!

The same goes for any bucket-carrying job. Once bucket carriers have used up their sick days and vacation days, if they can't continue to carry buckets, they won't continue to get a paycheck. Period.

No Buckets = No Pay

Dentist Can't Carry Buckets Anymore

Here's a real-life example. My previous dentist

was the best dentist I've ever had. She was a complete professional — a great chair-side manner. Great personality. Great technician — every visit was virtually pain free. Plus, she loved what she did, and she set her own hours (her office was open only three days a week so she could spend four-day weekends with her family).

She pulled down more than $100,000 a year working three days a week in a job she loved. This was a bucket-carrier's dream job if there ever was one.

One problem. Before the age of 40, she developed arthritis in her hands and couldn't work anymore. Today she teaches at a local university earning one-third of the income she earned as a dentist. Through no fault of her own, her dream job disappeared.

Now do you see why I say there's no such thing as a secure bucket-carrying job? Can you see how vulnerable bucket carriers are?

The problem with the Time-for-Money Trap is that if you can't trade the time, you don't get the money!

Pablo the Pipeline Man recognized the limitations of bucket carrying early on — and he set out to create a system whereby he could continue to get paid whether he put in more time or not.

Pablo understood that there's no security in bucket carrying. He understood that a pipeline is your lifeline.

What Would Happen to You If You Couldn't Put in the Time?

What about you — what would you do if your income stopped tomorrow?

What would happen if you got laid off?...

What would happen if you got sick or disabled and couldn't carry those buckets anymore?

What if a medical emergency ate up your savings?

What if your nest egg evaporated overnight?

If your income stopped tomorrow, how long could you pay the mortgage? ... make your car payments?... or pay for your kid's schooling?

Six months? Three months? Three weeks?!!!!

Your Nest Egg

6 months? 3 months? 3 weeks?

If disaster strikes, do you have a lifeline that would protect you and your family? Or are you gambling that bucket carrying will continue uninterrupted for as long as you need the income?

Whether you push a broom... push paper... or push a profession..., you're still trading one unit of time for one unit of money.

Where's the security in that?

Pipelines Pay While You Play

As Pablo said, *"There must be a better way!"*

Fortunately, there is.

It's called a pipeline — ongoing residual income — income that keeps coming in whether you put in the time or not. The only way to build true security is to do what Pablo did — build a pipeline while you're still carrying buckets!

Pipelines are lifelines because they enable people to escape the Time-for-Money Trap. When you build a pipeline, you do the work once, but you get paid over and over again.

Pipelines are open 24/7/365. Which means pipelines can pay you while you sleep. Or while you play. Or while you're retired. Or while you're sick and disabled and can't work. Or during emergencies.

That's the power of residual income.

That's why I say your pipelines are your lifelines!

Pipelines = Lifelines

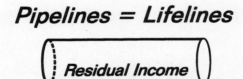

-23-

We Live in a Bucket-Carrying World

> "We've got a great job, Pablo. I can carry 100 buckets a day. At a penny a bucket, that's a dollar a day. I'm rich! By the end of the week, I can buy a new pair of shoes. By the end of the month, a cow. By the end of six months, I can buy a new hut. We have the best job in town. We have weekends off and two weeks' paid vacation every year. We're set for life! Get out of here with your pipeline."
>
> — from *The Parable of the Pipeline*

A doctor driving his four-year-old daughter to daycare left his stethoscope on the car seat. The daughter reached over and started to play with it.

"My daughter wants to follow in my footsteps," the doctor thought to himself. "This is the proudest moment of my life."

The child arranged the stethoscope around her neck and held the sensor in front of her like a microphone.

"Welcome to McDonald's. May I take your order?"

This cute story illustrates why we gravitate to bucket-carrying jobs — it's called "monkey see, monkey do." The little girl had been to McDonald's so often that she mistook the stethoscope for a headset and copycatted the way the employees talked to customers.

Like the little girl, most people mistake bucket carrying for pipeline building. We observe that 99% of the people carry buckets. So we naturally assume that bucket carrying is the only way to get what we want in life.

Bucket Carriers vs. Pipeline Builders

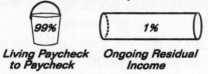

Living Paycheck to Paycheck   **Ongoing Residual Income**

That's why Bruno had such a tough time understanding the power of pipelines — Pablo was the first pipeline builder Bruno ever knew! Bruno rejected pipelines because they were different. To Bruno, pipelines were unproven. To Bruno, pipelines were radical and risky.

The vast majority of people think like Bruno. We grow up surrounded by broke bucket carriers, so we figure that's the way of the world. It reminds me of the bumper sticker I saw recently:

100,000 lemmings can't be wrong!

People think the same about bucket carrying — *100 million bucket carriers can't be wrong! Well, yes, they can.*

Lemming Mentality

Buying into Bucket Carrying

Let's face it — there are a lot more bucket carriers in this world than there are pipeline builders.

Why?

Because bucket carrying is the model that our parents followed and the one they taught us to follow. The bucket-carrying model tells you that in a bucket-carrying world, here's what you have to do to get ahead:

Go to school and learn how to carry buckets. Work really hard. Earn the right to carry bigger buckets. Resign from Bucket Company A to work for Bucket Company B, which lets you carry even bigger buckets. Work longer hours so you can carry more buckets. Put the kids through bucket-carrying college. Change careers from carrying metal buckets... to carrying plastic buckets... to carrying digital buckets. Dream of the day you can retire from bucket carrying. Until then, carry those buckets. Carry those buckets....

What do all those bucket carriers earn for their efforts?

Surprisingly little.

According to *Parade* magazine's annual "What People Earn" survey, the average worker in America earns $28,500 a year. Subtract almost 20% for taxes, and that leaves $22,500 to live on.

Let's face it — $22,500 take-home pay isn't enough money to cover the basic needs for a family of four. Which means the vast majority of people are desperate for more money!

Bucket Carriers' Average Pay

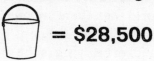 = $28,500

Buckets on Parade

So what do bucket carriers do when they need more money? Because they have a bucket-carrying mentality, they come up with a bucket-carrying solution — if you need more money, you've got to carry more buckets!

"*I'll get a second job carrying buckets in the evenings and weekends,*" Daddy Bucket Carrier says.

"I can go back to the bucket-carrying job I had before the kids were born," says Mommy Bucket Carrier.

"The kids can get bucket-carrying jobs after school and in the summer," the bucket-carrying parents announce.

And that's what they do. The result?

Today, North Americans work the longest hours in the world, even more than the work-obsessed Japanese. Is the earn-more-money-by-carrying-more-buckets plan working?

In a word, "NO!"

Here are the cold, hard facts:

- Consumer debt is at a record high. Household debt in the U.S. has more than quadrupled in the last 17 years. The average household today has 95¢ of debt for every dollar of disposable income.

- The proportion of women working to support their families more than doubled over the past 20 years, from 19% in 1980 to 46% today.

- More and more people are taking second and third mortgages on their single biggest asset — their homes — to pay bills.

- Personal bankruptcies have increased every year to 1.4 million in the year 2000 — even though the economy is booming!

Hello-o-o-o! What's wrong with this picture?

The Fallacy of Carrying Bigger Buckets

Bucket carriers reason that bigger buckets mean bigger paychecks. So bucket carriers tell themselves that everything would be okay if they could just get a job carrying bigger buckets.

Bucket carriers are forever wondering how much other bucket carriers earn. The U.S. Bureau of Labor Statistics keeps track of the hourly wages of hundreds of different occupations. How does your hourly wage compare to other jobs?

Hourly Wage
(from U.S. Bureau of Labor Statistics)

Occupation	Hourly Wage
Fast-food cook	$ 6.29
Gas station attendant	$ 7.34
Janitor	$ 8.44
Retail salesperson	$ 9.12
Secretary	$ 11.86
Roofer	$ 13.63
Car mechanic	$ 13.97
Truck driver	$ 14.08
Firefighter	$ 15.63
Mail carrier	$ 16.39
Loan officer	$ 20.05
Computer programmer	$ 25.67
Chemical engineer	$ 29.44
Physicist	$ 33.23
Lawyer	$ 36.49
Dentist	$ 44.40
Physicians, surgeons	$ 49.05

Assuming most people get paid for 40 hours a week (even though they probably *work at least 50 hours a week... or more!*) and get two weeks' paid vacation each year, here's the annual income for five of the above occupations:

Annual Income

1. Cook .... $ 13,083
2. Retail salesperson .... $ 18,970
3. Mail carrier .... $ 34,091
4. Lawyer .... $ 75,899
5. Physician $102,024

Now, if you were a cook... or a retail salesperson... or a mail carrier, you might look at the annual income of a lawyer or physician and think, "Wow, if I made that kind of money every year, I'd be financially free! No more lying awake at night worrying about paying the bills!"

Bucket Carriers' Income

| 28 K | 76 K | 102 K |
| Average Person | Lawyer's Income | Doctor's Income |

True, the physician's bucket is a lot bigger than a cook's bucket — about 10 times bigger! But that doesn't mean the physician is financially independent. He's just as dependent on his bucket-carrying job as the cook or the mail carrier.

Why? Simple — professionals make more than the average worker. *But they spend more!* Truth is, the doctors or lawyers making six figures a year are spending most of their income to support their lavish lifestyles.

Just compare an average worker's expenses to a professional's:

The average worker drives a $5,000 used car. The doctor or lawyer drives a $45,000 Lexus.

The average worker sends their kids to free public school. The doctor or lawyer pays for private school.

The average worker owns a $75,000 home. The doctor or lawyer owns a $350,000 home.

The average worker eats at Pizza Hut once a week. The doctor or lawyer eats out twice a week at ritzy restaurants.

The average worker can't afford to take a vacation. The doctor or lawyer takes the family skiing in Vail every year.

The average worker plays golf at a public course. The doctor or lawyer belongs to an expensive country club... or two.

You get the picture.

People envy doctors and lawyers and accountants because they get to carry huge buckets. True, the physician's bucket may be 10 times bigger than the cook's. But the physician spends 10 times more, so they both end up in the same predicament — living paycheck to paycheck!

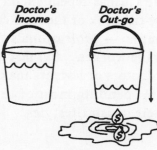

Doctor's Income   Doctor's Out-go

Buckets Eventually Dry Up

Thomas J. Stanley and William D. Danko, authors of the bestseller *The Millionaire Next Door*, observed that carrying big buckets is not the same as creating wealth. The authors came to this realization by surveying people who lived in upscale neighborhoods, assuming that people who drove expensive cars and lived in expensive homes were wealthy.

OOPS! — wrong assumption! Stanley and Danko came to this startling conclusion about wealth creation:

> *"Most people have it all wrong about wealth in America. Wealth is not the same as income. If you make a good income each year and spend it all, you are not getting wealthier. You are just living high. Wealth is what you accumulate, not what you spend.*
>
> *"How do you become wealthy? Here, too, most people have it wrong. It is seldom luck or inheritance or advanced degrees or even intelligence that enables people to amass fortunes. Wealth is more the result of a lifestyle of hard work, perseverance, planning, and, most of all, self-discipline."*

In other words, buckets, no matter how big they are, will eventually dry up. Pipelines, on the other hand, are self-sustaining. But pipelines require a sacrifice. Pipelines don't build themselves. You have to take the time and make the effort to build them.

Eventually All Buckets Dry Up

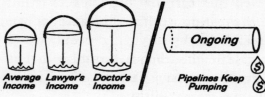

Average Income   Lawyer's Income   Doctor's Income   Pipelines Keep Pumping

Ongoing

A Bigger Bucket Won't Solve the Problem

Everybody would love to increase the size of their bucket. No one's going to turn down an annual raise or a better job with more pay. If bucket carrying is your only source of income, then I say carry the biggest bucket you can. That's only common sense.

But the fact remains that carrying buckets is never going to make you financially free. Carrying buckets will never make your family safe and secure — no matter how big your buckets! Why?

Because as long as you carry buckets, you have to show up and do the work in order to get paid. The day you stop carrying buckets, that's the day the money stops coming in!

- **Illness or Injury**
- **Layoffs**
- **Retirement**

Many a bucket carrier has gone from the

"millionaire next door" to the "bankrupt guy next door" because he neglected to build pipelines while he was carrying buckets. When his bucket dried up, so did his lifestyle.

"Pipelines are your lifelines," my father used to say.

Are you beginning to see why?

PART 2

Your Pipelines Are Your Lifelines

LESSON THREE

The Power of the Pipeline

> But Pablo was not easily discouraged. He patiently explained his pipeline plan to his best friend. Pablo would work part of the day carrying buckets and then part of the day and weekends building his pipeline.
>
> He knew it would be hard work digging a ditch in the rocky soil. He also knew it would take a year, possibly two, before his pipeline would start to pay big dividends.
>
> But Pablo believed in his dream, and he went to work.
>
> — from *The Parable of the Pipeline*

This is the tale of two polar opposites — a big-time baseball player and a small town elementary school teacher.

They couldn't be more different — one was a young man and one was an elderly woman. One was paid millions a year and the other never earned more than $10,000. One lived his life in the spotlight. The other lived her life in a small town in Massachusetts.

But these were only small differences compared to the personal and financial choices each made. You see, one of the people you're going to read about built pipelines and retired a multi-millionaire. The other stayed a bucket carrier and, as I write this, is teetering on the brink of bankruptcy.

The stories are about two very different people, but that's not what's important. What's important is the choices they made and the lessons you can learn from those choices. After you hear these two tales, it should be crystal clear why building pipelines is the only way to create true security and true financial freedom.

Your Choices

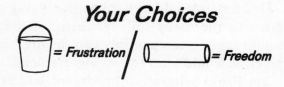

= Frustration / = Freedom

The Ballad of the Ball Player

Let's begin with the tale of the famous baseball player. Over the years, this talented athlete has made some bad choices, both personally and financially.

His personal choices have led to a broken marriage, alcohol abuse, and drug addiction. That's bad enough. But his financial choices have been just as bad, for he's also broke. I'm sure you've heard of this athlete. He's been in the spotlight for almost 20 years now.

His name is Darryl Strawberry. His story is a cautionary tale for what you should NOT do in order to achieve financial freedom.

Darryl Strawberry has been playing professional baseball for almost half of his life. The 38-year-old outfielder broke into the major leagues when he was still a teenager and was immediately hailed as the "next Ted Williams."

Strawberry has made a fortune during his career — somewhere between $2 and $5 million a year. And that's just from playing baseball. Add another couple million a year from endorsements, personal appearances, speeches, and autograph signings, and he's earned $50 to $100 million before his 40th birthday.

Strawberries Don't Field Forever

A guy making that kind of money has to be set for life, right?

Wrong.

According to a local newspaper report, "Strawberry has no income or savings to support his current wife, Charisse, and their three children..."

$100 million and not a thing to show for it. What happened?

He spent it.

Expensive houses. Expensive cars. Expensive lawyers to defend his run-ins with the law. Expensive divorce. Expensive drug and alcohol rehabilitation clinics.

As I write this, Strawberry has been suspended from playing baseball. Which means he has no income coming in. The only thing still coming in are the bills. And they come in day after day, month after month, as steady as the rain in a monsoon.

Big Income + Bigger Out-go = **Disaster!**

How to Become the Millionaire Next Door

The second tale has a much different ending. It's the tale of a small town teacher named Margaret O'Donnell, and it proves that you don't have to carry big buckets in order to build big pipelines.

Ms. O'Donnell taught school for more than 50 years. When she retired in her 70s, she was making around $8,500 a year. When she died at age 100, she left almost $2 million to 10 different charities, including her church, schools she attended, and a Boy Scout troop.

How could a woman earning less than $10,000 a year accumulate a small fortune? Simple. She built a long-term investment pipeline by making regular monthly investments in quality stocks and allowing them to compound over time.

Building Long-Term Pipelines

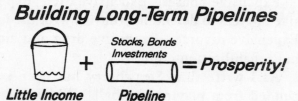

Little Income + Stocks, Bonds Investments Pipeline = **Prosperity!**

"Margaret enjoyed stocks," said her broker, Bob Wolanske. "The first time I met her, she threw three papers on my desk and said, 'What should I do with these dogs?,' referring to some stocks that weren't doing well."

Over the next 20 years, Margaret's portfolio bloomed to include a collection of blue chip stocks, tax-exempt bonds, and utility stocks that she held until her death. She rarely touched any of her investments, enabling her retirement pipeline to grow year after year after year.

Small Sacrifices, Big Results

Now, in case you're thinking that Margaret was one of those penny-pinching spinsters who clipped coupons and saved used tea bags, you'd be wrong. She ate out often with friends. Drove a late-model Buick. And frequently flew to Europe to enjoy long vacations.

She didn't deny herself the pleasures of life. But she also showed discipline and restraint in her spending. And she saved and invested each and every month, even in retirement.

You see, Margaret was the classic example of a long-term pipeline builder. She started saving and investing in her early 20s. And she continued right up until her death at age 100 (as you'll learn in the coming chapters, pipelines grow bigger and bigger over time).

Growing Your Pipelines

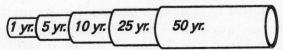

Like Pablo, pipeline builders may not have much to show for their efforts during the first few days or even years. But consistent, disciplined efforts over time can transform small contributions into huge dividends.

Pipelines Keep Pumping After Buckets Run Dry

Now do you understand what I mean when I talk about the power of the pipeline? Darryl Strawberry has carried a huge bucket for years. And what does he have to show for it today? Nothing but boxes of cancelled checks!

Strawberry has had 20 years to build pipelines. If he had taken just 10% of his earnings and put the money to work by building an investment pipeline in the stock market, he could've had a lifeline worth between $20 million and $100 million by now.

But he didn't.

Missed Opportunity

No Pipeline Means No Residual Income

Strawberry assumed his big bucket would never dry up. Wrong assumption. Buckets don't automatically replenish themselves, no matter how big they are. That's because the bucket carrier has to lug the bucket to get it refilled.

When he stops lugging — either through retirement... or illness... or injury... or burnout — the bucket starts drying up.

Pipelines, on the other hand, keep pumping profits long after buckets run dry. That rule holds true for big bucket carriers, just as it does for small bucket carriers. As I said, it's not the size of the bucket that counts. People with big buckets tend to be big spenders. The key to financial freedom is to adopt a pipeline building mentality — and then to put your pipeline plan into action!

Big Bucket Model

Big bucket   Big expenses   Small assets

The Smaller the Bucket, the Bigger the Need for a Pipeline

Earning a lot of money doesn't guarantee financial independence. Only pipelines can do that. If you don't adopt a pipeline strategy, your bucket will eventually dry up!

I tell you the story of Darryl Strawberry to exaggerate a point — namely, if a bucket as big as Darryl Strawberry's can dry up, what about yours?

Think about it. Strawberry lived from paycheck to paycheck.

What about you?

Strawberry acted as if his bucket-carrying days would never end.

What about you?

Strawberry foolishly spent money and wasted time when he could have been using it wisely to build a lifeline.

What about you?

What About You?

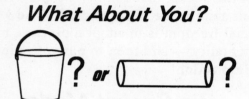

Sure, Strawberry made some bad choices that cost him a lot of money. But his worst financial choice was his failure to build pipelines. That's unforgivable! What was he thinking?

Margaret O'Donnell, on the other hand, had the wisdom to build pipelines while she was still carrying buckets. When her bucket-carrying days came to an end, her pipelines kept pumping and the cash kept flowing.

It's Your Turn to Choose

Now I ask you, which financial situation would you rather be in — Darryl Strawberry's? Or Margaret O'Donnell's? If the answer is Margaret O'Donnell's, then you need to start building your pipelines right away!

Pipelines are lifelines because they're self-sustaining. They may need priming from time to time. And repairs. Perhaps even rebuilding. But pipelines can keep pumping profits year after year.

Your Choice

"Your choices, not chance, determine your destiny."

Both Darryl Strawberry and Margaret O'Donnell had a choice. Darryl Strawberry chose buckets. Margaret O'Donnell chose pipelines.

They made their choices.

Now it's your turn to choose.

Leverage: The Power Behind the Pipeline

> Once the pipeline was complete, Pablo didn't have to carry buckets anymore. The water flowed whether he worked or not. It flowed while he ate. It flowed while he slept. It flowed on the weekends while he played. The more the water flowed into the village, the more the money flowed into Pablo's pockets!
>
> — from *The Parable of the Pipeline*

Leverage is an awesome concept — a civilization-altering concept.

In fact, without leverage, you wouldn't be holding this book right now!

Let me explain.

In 1440, a young German entrepreneur named Johannes Gutenberg converted a wine press into the world's first commercial printing press. He printed 180 copies of the *Gutenberg Bible* and sold them all within a few days.

Gutenberg's printing press was an immediate success. Within decades, printing presses had sprung up all over Europe. By the mid-1600s, there were eight million printed books circulating in Europe, which was 10 times the number of books that had been produced during the previous thousands of years combined!

Books by Bucket Carriers vs. Publishing by Pipeline Builders

The Gutenberg press shattered the books-by-bucket-carriers paradigm. Prior to Gutenberg, books were hand-copied by scribes and monks. One hand-written book could take years to produce and were so expensive that only royalty could afford them.

Gutenberg changed all that. With the printing press, the printer set the movable type once... and then could easily produce thousands of exact copies. The printing press leveraged the printer's time and money, thereby dramatically increasing productivity.

In the books-by-bucket-carriers model, there's a one-to-one ratio between efforts and results. One hour's effort produces one hour's result. If it took one scribe one day to hand copy one page, then it would have taken him 100 days to turn out 100 pages.

Enter the printing press — the pipeline-building model. Let's say it took a 16th century printer one day to

Books by Hand Model

One hour = one page

set the type for one page, so that by the end of the day, he would have produced just one printer's proof copy.

But look what happened in day two: The printer came into work and pressed 100 copies! In other words, a printer could produce in two days what it would have taken the scribe 100 days to produce. That's the power of leverage!

Printing Press Model

1 hour = 100 pages

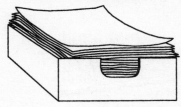

In the pipeline-building model, the ratio between effort and result is no longer 1:1. When we use leverage, the effort remains the same, but the result can be 100 times greater... 1,000 times greater... or even millions of times greater!

Two Kinds of Leverage: Time and Money

The root word for leverage — *lever* — comes from an old French word meaning "to make lighter," which is an apt description of the power of leverage. By employing a lever, a big load can be made so light that a child could easily move it.

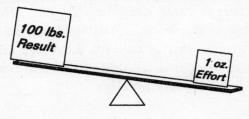

When we apply the principle of leverage to time and money, the same thing happens — the results are compounded.

For example, in the case of leveraging time, one hour's effort can result in 100 hours of production. One week's work can result in one year's production.

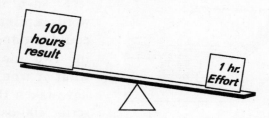

In the case of leveraging money, each dollar invested over time can compound until it grows to many times the initial investment.

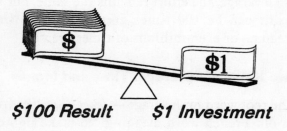

$100 Result $1 Investment

Classic Examples of Leverage

The printing press is an example of how people can leverage their time, money, and efforts. Leverage shatters the equation of one unit of time for one unit of money. Leverage allows people to work smarter, not harder, and it's the power behind every pipeline.

Leveraging Time: Hiring employees is a classic example of how people can leverage their time. Let's say you want to open a restaurant. It would be impossible for you to act as the host... waiter... chef... dishwasher... and book-keeper and still run a profitable business. You can only be in one place at a time, so you hire people to perform certain tasks.

If you pay your 10-person staff an average of $10 per hour, you're paying out $100 an hour in wages. If your restaurant takes in an average of $1,000 per hour in revenue, the difference after expenses goes into your pocket.

*Leveraging Time
in a Small Business*

Leveraging Money: A classic example of leveraging money is investing in the stock market. No doubt you've heard of Warren Buffett. He's a living legend on Wall Street and the second or third richest man in the world. He built his fortune the old-fashioned way — he leveraged other people's money and made himself and his investors rich in the process.

How rich? Check this out. If you had invested $10,000 in Buffett's Berkshire

Hathaway stock back in 1965 and left it there to grow year after year, by 1998 your investment would have been worth — hang on to your hat — *$51 million!* Wow! How would you like to own that pipeline?!!

Thirty-five years ago, one share of Berkshire Hathaway stock cost only $19. By the end of 1998, that single share was worth about $70,000. Which means that you could have leveraged a $300 investment in 1965 into $1 million today! Unbelievable!

Leveraging $ in Berkshire Hathaway

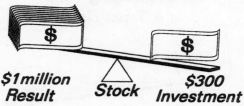

$1 million Result △ **Stock** **$300 Investment**

Pipelines Are Worth Building

Now do you understand the power of leverage? Berkshire Hathaway stock is living proof that with leverage, the results are disproportionate to the effort!

Think about it — how much effort would it have taken to accumulate $300 back in 1965? Two or three days' work... maybe a week's work at the most. Just imagine — once the $300 was invested, you wouldn't have to do any more work because your pipeline was already built.

The only other work you'd have to do is check the stock prices in the newspaper every now and then.

Ask yourself — wouldn't it be great if you could turn $300 into $1 million without having to lift a finger?

Can you see how the wise use of leverage can multiply a little money or a little time a thousand times over?

Doesn't it make sense to find a mechanism whereby you could leverage $1 into $100?... or one hour into 100 hours?

Wouldn't it be great to do the work once and let leverage do the rest!

Folks, if you'd like to enjoy the benefits of leverage, then you need to do what pipeline builders such as Pablo and Warren Buffett did — find a mechanism to leverage your time and money today... and *enjoy a big reward tomorrow!*

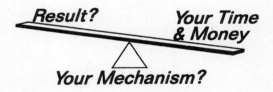

Money Leverage:
The Palm Beach Pipeline

"Just think," Pablo continued. "We could make a small percentage of every gallon of water that goes through those pipelines. The more water that flows through the pipelines, the more money that will flow into our pockets. The pipeline I built isn't the end of a dream. It's only the beginning!"

— from *The Parable of the Pipeline*

Legend has it that one of the ancient emperors of China fell in love with a new game called "chess." The emperor decided to reward the game's creator. He summoned the inventor to the royal palace and announced to the court that the inventor would be granted one wish.

"I am honored, Your Highness," the inventor muttered humbly. "My wish is that you grant me one grain of rice."

"Just one grain of rice?" the startled emperor asked.

"Well, just one grain for the first square of the chessboard," the inventor said. "Then doubling to two grains for the second square... four grains for the third square... and so on until the single grain has been doubled for the entire chess board. That is my simple wish."

The emperor was well pleased. "I have been given such a wonderful game at such a cheap price," he thought to himself. "My ancestors have smiled upon me today."

"It is done!" the emperor cried. "Bring out the chess board and let everyone here witness our agreement."

The court gathered around the chess board. A kitchen servant produced a one-pound bag of rice and handed it to the inventor, who smiled as he opened the bag.

"I suggest you return to the kitchen for a larger bag," the inventor said to the servant. The court laughed loudly, mistaking his comment for sarcasm. Then the inventor began placing the grains of rice on the board, doubling the number of grains as he went:

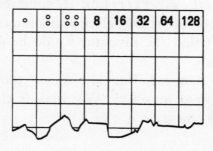

The onlookers laughed and nudged each other as the first row of eight squares was filled... 1... 2... 4... 8... 16... 32... 64... 128 grains of rice. But the giggles soon gave way to gasps by the middle of the second row, for small piles of rice soon doubled to small bags of rice... which doubled to medium-sized bags of rice... which doubled again to big bags of rice.

○	○○	○○ ○○	8	16	32	64	128
256	512	1K	2K	4K	8K	16K	32K
....	....	....	....	....	....	....	....
....	....	....	....	....	....	....	....
....	....	....	....	....	....	....	....

By the end of the second row, the emperor knew he had made a huge mistake. The grains owed to the inventor totaled 32,768 — *and there were 48 squares remaining!*

The emperor stopped the game and called in the land's wisest mathematicians. They tossed the beads of their abacuses and made hasty markings on slate boards. After much fussing, the mathematicians reached a unanimous conclusion:

A grain of rice doubled for every square on the 64-square chess board would calculate to *18 million trillion grains of rice — a quantity equal to all the rice in the world multiplied by 10!*

The emperor halted the demonstration and made the inventor an offer he couldn't refuse — if the emperor were released from his word, the inventor would receive a country estate with hun-

dreds of acres of fertile rice fields. The inventor
gladly accepted. Everyone toasted the inventor
and congratulated him on his wisdom and clever-
ness. And he happily retired to his estate, enjoying many, many years in splendid comfort.

The Doubling Concept: Eighth Wonder of the World

The story of the emperor and the inventor
teaches us the power of the doubling concept.
This concept has been around since the first
bank paid the first wealthy merchant interest
on a deposit, so it's time-tested and proven.

The inventor and the emperor's mathematicians may have been the first people to recog-
nize the power of duplication, but they certainly
weren't the last. Centuries later another famous
mathematician named Albert Einstein recognized the awesome power of duplication, or
"compounding," as it's sometimes referred to,
calling it "the eighth wonder of the world."

The doubling concept has become such a
cornerstone of wealth creation that I call it "the
Palm Beach Pipeline," named after the ritzy city
in Florida where hundreds of the world's richest heirs own sprawling estates overlooking the
Atlantic Ocean.

The rich people in Palm Beach don't have to
work for money. *They make money work for them!*
How? They invest large amounts of inherited
money in pipelines that churn out huge profits
year in and year out, whether the investors work

or not.

Palm Beach Pipelines are fueled by the doubling concept, which means the lucky heirs can enjoy a fabulous lifestyle... while they get richer in the process! That's what I call having your cake and eating it, too.

The Rule of 72: The Rule of the Rich

To better understand how rich people get richer, let's take a look at "The Rule of 72," a mind-boggling wealth-building concept that the world's top investment brokers teach their rich clients. The Rule of 72 is a simple formula for calculating how many years it would take for an investment to double. Here's the way it works.

Doubling Concept or Rule of 72

1) Determine the annual interest rate on your investment
2) Divide the interest rate into 72
3) The result is the number of years it takes for your investment to double

---

For example, let's say an heiress invests $100,000 in a stock that pays an annual return of 10% per year. Here's the Rule of 72 in action:

Rule of 72 in Action

Step 1: $100,000 original investment
Step 2: 10% annual return
Step 3: 72 divided by 10 = 7.2 years
Payoff: $100,000 would become $200,000 in 7.2 years

If the heiress didn't spend the profits or her principle, the original investment of $100,000 would double to $200,000 in 7.2 years... to $400,000 in 14.4 years... to $800,000 in 21.6 years... and $1.6 million in 28.8 years... and on and on. As you can see, the longer the money is allowed to compound, the bigger the size of the pipeline.

By leveraging the power of compounding, people who inherit million-dollar fortunes can live like royalty and still leave an even bigger fortune for their children!

The magic of compounding is the reason that thousands of heirs named Kennedy... DuPont... Firestone... Ford... Rockefeller... and Getty can continue to live a life of luxury without their fortunes drying up. In effect, their bucket never runs dry because the pipeline keeps pumping year after year, for decades, or in the case of the Rothschild heirs in Europe, for more than two centuries!

Kids and Money

Fortunately, pipelines built by leveraging money aren't reserved just for rich people. Average people can take advantage of the doubling concept, too, as we learned from the story about Margaret O'Donnell, a low-paid school teacher who amassed several million dollars by leveraging her money in the stock market.

So, how do average people leverage their money to create a long-term pipeline?

The best way to answer that is to tell you about

a powerful little book called *Kids and Money* by Michael J. Searls. Actually, the book could be titled *People and Money*, because the principles outlined by Searls apply to young and old alike.

Searls, a former power broker on Wall Street and father of four, recommends a simple system to teach kids to manage their money more responsibly.

He suggests that parents get three plastic jars and label jar one "spend & give," jar two "save," and jar three "invest." When parents give their children their allowance for the week, they divide the money equally into the three jars.

Kids & Money System

Spend & Give   Save   Invest

The "spend and give" jar is for immediate spending — bubble gum, baseball cards, etc. It's also money to be used for tithing and charity.

The "save" jar is for spending on bigger ticket items, such as a new CD or video game.

The "invest" jar differs from the first two in that it's not for spending. Ever. Searls calls this jar "...the most important component, because if we don't have something to put away for a rainy day, the threat of debt will always hover above our heads."

Adults who are serious about building long-term investment pipelines need to start managing their money according to a three-jar system. But instead of putting their money into jars, they should put it into bank and brokerage accounts.

Adults & Money System

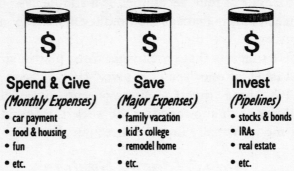

Spend & Give	Save	Invest
(Monthly Expenses)	*(Major Expenses)*	*(Pipelines)*
• car payment	• family vacation	• stocks & bonds
• food & housing	• kid's college	• IRAs
• fun	• remodel home	• real estate
• etc.	• etc.	• etc.

Pay Yourself First!

The key to leveraging your money like rich people do is to "pay yourself first" by making regular monthly contributions into investment accounts — and then leaving the money to compound!

The best way to fund your investment pipelines is to take some money out of your income bucket each month and deposit it into your pipelines.

Building a Long-Term Pipeline

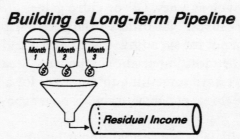

How Average People Become Millionaires

Too bad we weren't able to choose rich parents — then we wouldn't have to worry about "forced savings plans" and automatic payroll deductions.

But the truth is, the vast majority of millionaires in this country didn't inherit their fortunes. Statistics show that four out of five millionaires never inherited more than $10,000. But what they did do was copy the investment strategies of the Rockefellers and the Kennedys.

In a word, self-made millionaires leveraged their money to build their own Palm Beach Pipelines! How? By using the "three jar system" — instead of spending every dime they make, they put aside a big chunk of their income in the "invest jar," and let it compound year after year.

Typically, millionaires save 15% to 20% of their gross income and invest it wisely in asset-building pipelines, such as stocks, bonds, closely-held businesses, rental property, commercial real estate, pension funds, and the like.

That's why most millionaires don't hit the million-dollar mark until they're in their 50s or 60s — it can take decades before compounding really kicks into high gear. Ten thousand dollars at 10% doubles to $20,000 after seven years... but in 50 years it will double seven times, *which calculates to almost $1.3 million!*

Power of Compounding
$10,000 @ 10% Interest

Year 1	7	14	21	28	35	42	49
$10,000	20 K	40 K	80 K	160 K	320 K	640 K	1.3 M

If You Don't Have the Money, What Do You Have to Leverage?

Wouldn't it be great to be a millionaire?

You can, you know. And you don't have to win the lottery to do it.

The Millionaire's Club used to be a very exclusive club. You had to be born into the right family. Go to the right schools.

That's not the case anymore. Today, average people can join the Millionaire's Club, too. It's open to anyone with the discipline to invest a regular portion of their income and let it compound over time.

But let's face it — not everyone has the patience to spend 40 or 50 years building their retirement pipeline. And not everyone has the money to build a Palm Beach Pipeline overnight.

Wouldn't it be great if there were a 5-year pipeline plan whereby average people could create ongoing residual income without having to invest a small fortune?

Well, there is a 5-year pipeline plan available. Best of all, you don't need lots of money to build this pipeline. Because instead of leveraging your money... *you leverage your time!*

Time Leverage:
The People's Pipeline

> While Bruno lay in his hammock on evenings and weekends, Pablo kept digging his pipeline. The first few months, Pablo didn't have much to show for his efforts. The work was hard — even harder than Bruno's because Pablo was working evenings and weekends, too.
>
> But Pablo kept reminding himself that tomorrow's dreams are built on today's sacrifices. Day by day he dug, an inch at a time.
> — from *The Parable of the Pipeline*

There's an old Appalachian expression that sums up the difference between money leverage and time leverage. It goes like this:

There are two ways to get to the top of a giant oak tree. You can sit on an acorn and wait. Or you can climb it.

When people leverage their money over decades to build pipelines, they're choosing to sit on an acorn and wait. I call this the "50-Year Pipeline Plan." This is what compounding is all about — waiting patiently while your money doubles again and again over the years.

There's no question that the 50-Year Pipeline Plan works. Remember how Margaret O'Donnell's pipeline transformed her from a underpaid teacher to a multi-millionaire?!!!

Like Margaret O'Donnell, I'm also a big believer in building long-term pipelines. Over the years, I've leveraged a portion of my income to build "Palm Beach Pipelines" in everything from pension funds... to stock market accounts... to IRAs... to real estate. It's called diversification. It's called building lifelines.

50-Year Pipeline Plan

- Ⓢ CDs & T-Bills
- Ⓢ Pension Funds
- Ⓢ Stocks & Bonds
- Ⓢ Your Home
- Ⓢ Social Security
- Ⓢ 401 (k)
- Ⓢ IRAs
- Ⓢ Real Estate

But I'm also a big believer in climbing oak trees!
I call climbing oak trees the "5-Year Pipeline Plan." It accomplishes the same goal as the 50-Year Pipeline Plan — financial independence and security. *But it only takes 10% of the time!*

That's why I've spent time, money, and effort in building several fast-growing businesses. Instead of having to wait 50 years to get to the top of the tree, I can build a business that gets me there in two to five years.

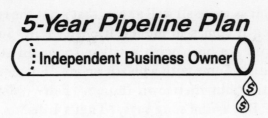

5-Year Pipeline Plan

Independent Business Owner

Time Levels the Playing Field

The beauty of time leverage is that we've all been given the same amount of time. Which means time levels the playing field between rich people and average income earners. Whether you're Donald Trump... or Donald the dump truck driver... everyone has been given the same amount of time each day.

That's why I call time leverage the "People's Pipeline." Time is available in equal amounts to everyone, whether they're rich or poor... man or woman... black or white... college educated or high school dropout... young or old. You can't say that about money, now can you?

Think of it this way. Wouldn't it be great if you and everyone else could start every single day with $1,440 in your personal bank account? The money would be yours and yours alone and no one could tell you what to do with it. You could spend it... invest it... blow it... burn it... give it away... leverage it... or waste it, knowing that the next morning, you'd wake up with another $1,440 in your account. If everyone could start off every day with $1,440, it would be a better, more fair world, wouldn't it?

But as we're all well aware, that's not the case. When it comes to money, life isn't fair. Some people are born with a silver spoon in their mouths. Some with a plastic spoon. Some with nothing but their own thumb. Fair? Maybe not. But as the song says, "That's Life."

We don't all start every day with $1,440 in our bank accounts — that's for sure. As for time — that's a different matter. *We DO all start every day with 1,440 minutes in our time account* (24 hours a day times 60 minutes an hour).

Since we all get the same amount of time, the difference between people who live paycheck to paycheck and people who are financially free is how they use their daily allotment of 1,440 minutes!

Personal Time Account

DATE: _____	Checking Account	DATE _____
TO: *Each day*	Pay to:	$ _____
FOR: _____	*1,440 minutes each day*	

You've Got More Time Than You Think

Some people put off building their pipelines because "right now is a bad time for me." Guess what — right now is a bad time for everybody! We're all stressed. We're all busy. We're all putting out fires and dealing with unexpected emergencies. There's a word for these bad times.

It's called life!

Some people waste their lives waiting for the "perfect time" to do x, y, or z. Well, they'll die waiting, because there's no such thing as a perfect time. If someone told you he'd give you $1 million if you'd sit in a corner and knit for two hours every day for a year, you'd find the time to knit, wouldn't you?

It wouldn't matter if your son broke his arm on the playground or your car wouldn't start after work. Rather than forfeit $1 million, you'd find the time to knit for two hours, perfect time or no perfect time. Humorist Art Buchwald put it this way: *"Whether it's the best of times or the worst of times, it's the only time we got."*

Sadly, most people take time for granted, especially small amounts of time. We've been conditioned to measure time in days and weeks and years, instead of minutes and hours. We work 9 to 5, Monday through Friday. We plan our lives according to a monthly calendar. We celebrate our birthdays and anniversaries once a year.

But the amazing thing about time is how a few minutes here and there every day can add up to huge chunks of time! For example, did you know how much total time the average person spends eating during their lifetimes? Would you guess a year? Two years? The answer is six years! Isn't that amazing? Here are some other short daily tasks that add up to huge blocks of time:

Total Time We Spend on Small Daily Tasks During Our Lifetime

6 years .... eating
5 years .... waiting in line
4 years .... cleaning house
3 years .... preparing meals
2 years .... trying to return phone calls
1 year .... searching for misplaced items
8 months .... opening junk mail
6 months .... sitting at red lights

By my tally, that's close to 22 years out of your lifetime! Which goes to prove that 15 minutes here... half an hour there... two hours there... can add up to huge blocks of time!

A Few Hours Can Turn into a Few Months

Just think for a moment what we could accomplish in our lives if we used a couple hours each evening and on the weekends to do something purposeful, like building a pipeline. If you set aside two hours each workday — let's say one in the morning before work and one in the evening — and three more hours on both Saturday and Sunday, you could add 16 hours of productive time a week to your schedule!

Sixteen hours a week over 50 weeks a year comes to 800 extra hours a year... which calculates to 100 eight-hour days... or three months and 10 days of extra eight-hour workdays each year! And all you had to do was set aside a couple of hours a day to get three extra months of productive time each year. Amazing, isn't it?

Productive Free Time

(2 hours/day) x (5 days) = 10 hours/week
(3 hours/Sat. & Sun.)　　= 6 hours/week
_____

　　　　　total extra time:　16 hours/week

Time Is Money

Now, I'm going to let you in on a little secret — using free time productively is one of the keys to why successful people have more, do more, and get more in life! Do you think Bill Gates comes home at 5:00 PM every day and watches seven hours of TV like the average American male does?

I don't think so....

A recent article in the *Wall Street Journal* states that the top 10% of earners in North America work an average of 52 hours a week, whereas those in the bottom 10% of earners work only 45 hours a week.

Not only do the top 10%-ers work longer — *they work smarter!* In other words, they don't trade their time for dollars. You won't walk into a convenience store and see Michael Jordan behind the counter selling customers lottery tickets and quarts of beer. Successful people in every line of work value their time, and they seek every opportunity to leverage their time!

Waste Not, Want Not

People often ask me why they should take the time and effort to build pipelines when things are going so well right at the moment. They tell me they deserve to relax after a hard day at the office. They reward themselves by leaning back in the La-Z-Boy recliner and watching TV until bedtime.

"Life is good," they tell me. "Got a good job. Got a few bucks in the bank. Kids are doing well in school. No need to rock the boat."

That's when I tell them that there's no better time to build your pipeline than when things are going great. Why? Because when the tide turns, it may be too late!

Then I tell them this old joke: A man was on the 30th floor of a fancy hotel overlooking Central Park in Manhattan. He pulled back the shades and threw open the window to enjoy the view. As he leaned out the window, he was startled to see a man falling past his room.

"How you doing?" he asked the falling man.

"*Fine — so far*," came the reply.

The point is that there are lots of bucket carriers in this world who are doing fine — *so far*. But they can't stay in a free-fall forever. As long as people trade time for dollars, there's no safety net in their lives. Why? Because when they can't put in the time due to illness... or injury... or layoffs, their paychecks will stop.

For bucket carriers, no paycheck means no security!

Financial Security

No Paycheck = No Security

The Fable of the Ant and the Grasshopper

As I write this, consumer confidence is high. Unemployment is low. Incomes are rising. Home sales are at record highs. Car sales are booming. Lots of people are fine — *so far.*

But we can't fall into the trap of mistaking "so far" for "forever." Everybody knows that life goes in cycles. So does the economy. Right now the business cycle is nearing its zenith. Your personal life cycle may be at an all-time high, too.

But what goes up, must come down. And when people start coming down, some of them are going to crash into some hard realities: Layoffs. Career changes. Credit card debt. Medical emergencies. Nursing home care for elderly parents.

Smart people understand that the best time to feather their nest is while business is booming. Smart people erect safety nets before a recession starts, not during! That's why I tell people that today is the best time to build their pipelines, not when the economy hits the skids.

It's like the fable of the ant and the grasshopper. The ant was a pipeline builder. He spent part of his summer days storing away grain for the coming winter. He enjoyed the summer, too.

But he had the wisdom to spend some of his time building his pipeline.

The grasshopper, on the other hand, was a bucket carrier. He spent all of his money as soon as he got it and wasted all of his time playing in the sunshine. He ignored the coming winter. When the cold winter came, he had no pipeline in place. And he starved to death.

Pay Me Now... Or Pay Me Later!

Do you remember the famous advertising slogan, *"Pay me now... or pay me later?"* The same goes for building pipelines. You can "pay a little now" by investing some of your time and money to build your pipelines today.... or you can "pay a lot later" by struggling to survive on a small Social Security check when you're in your 60s and 70s.

Just think — if your pipelines are in place, instead of having to pay later... *you'll get paid later!*

What a concept!

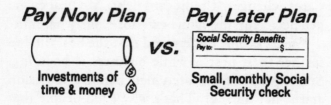

Pay Now Plan	vs.	Pay Later Plan
Investments of time & money		Small, monthly Social Security check

Time Leverage: The People's Pipeline

Remember — time levels the playing field!

We all DO NOT have the same amount of money to leverage.

But we all DO have the same amount of time!

By leveraging some of your leisure time wisely, you can build a pipeline that will continue to pay for years!

We're lucky to be living in an age when virtually anyone can leverage their time to build pipelines. That hasn't always been the case.

At the turn of the 20th century, only the very rich had the luxury of leveraging their time. In 1890, the vast majority of people worked 10 hours a day as laborers. They were too busy trying to stay alive to think about leverage.

But today more people have more free time than ever before in history. And time is the great equalizer! Time enables the little guy to compete with the big boys. Rich people don't get 48 hours a day while poor people get 12. They both get equal amounts of time — 24 hours a day, 7 days a week, 365 days a year.

The Greatest Time-Leveraging Tool in History

Today, pipelines are no longer the province of the rich. Anyone with a little time... and a lot of drive... can leverage their time to build a "people's pipeline" in two to five years that will flow for years — or even decades!

In fact, we have right at our fingertips the greatest time-leveraging tool in the history of the world! This time-leveraging tool has created more millionaires in less time than any other single invention in history.

I call this amazing tool the "e-pipeline," and

it's the ultimate tool for time leverage. You probably know the e-pipeline by a different name — a name that is flashed across newspaper headlines and TV screens 24 hours a day.

That name?

The Internet.

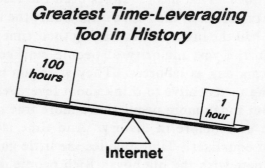

Greatest Time-Leveraging Tool in History

PART 3

The Ultimate Pipeline

LESSON SEVEN

e-compounding:
The Ultimate Pipeline

> Pablo the Pipeline Man became known as Pablo the Miracle Maker. Politicians lauded him for his vision and begged him to run for mayor. But Pablo understood that what he had accomplished wasn't a miracle. It was merely the first stage of a big, big dream. You see, Pablo had plans that reached far beyond his village.
>
> Pablo planned to build pipelines all over the world!
>
> — from *The Parable of the Pipeline*

Up to this point, we've talked about how people can leverage their time and money to build pipelines of ongoing residual income.

The question is, *"What is the most powerful and productive pipeline in the New Economy?"*

The answer is the Internet, a breakthrough technology I call "the e-pipeline of the New Economy." Folks, the Internet is transforming the way the world lives, works, and plays. In a word, the Internet is the future — *and the future is now!*

In this chapter I'll show you how you can take advantage of the greatest leveraging tool in history — the Internet — *to create a pipeline of ongoing residual income that you can build in two to five years, instead of 50 years!*

The Internet Revolution Is Just Beginning

The Internet Age is revolutionizing the world, that's for sure.

Jack Welch, CEO of General Electric, told *The Wall Street Journal* that the Internet was the greatest change in business in his lifetime — and Welch was born in 1936!

Andy Grove, the Chairman of Intel, was even more direct in his assessment: "In five years, every company will be an Internet company — or they won't be a company at all."

It's a Wired, Wired World After All

What makes the Internet pipeline so powerful?

Well, think for a moment what the Internet really is — it's millions of people all over the globe... each connected via a computer or cell phone... able to instantly communicate with — or sell to — each other 24/7/365... all for the price of a local telephone call.

It's mind-boggling!

The Internet is as fast as the speed of light... costs a few dollars a day to use... is always on... has limitless applications... and interconnects the world. Oh — and 100 million people were wired to the Web in less than half the time it took to build the Brooklyn Bridge. By 2003, more than one billion people will be online... purchasing $1 trillion of products and services via e-commerce.

That's not hype — that's a global revolution!

The Internet

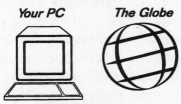

Your PC   **The Globe**

1 Billion People Online
e-commerce = $1 Trillion+ a Year

The Problem with the Internet

The Internet is truly revolutionary — but it's far from perfect.

In fact, the Internet has a problem. A BIG PROBLEM!

The Internet's biggest strength is also its biggest weakness — it's too big! Too crowded. Too confusing. Too competitive. Too hi-tech. Where do you shop? How do you buy? Who do you trust?

It's overwhelming!

According to the experts, e-commerce sites are facing three major challenges:

1) They need more traffic.
2) They need more sales.
3) They need more repeat business.

The Internet Needs Loyal Customers

In a nutshell, most e-commerce sites are hurting for customers — loyal customers. By "loyal" customers I mean people who have a reason to buy from an e-commerce site week after week and month after month, instead of once in a blue moon.

We hear a lot of talk about how many "hits" a website gets. But hits don't bring in revenue. Hits are like the members of walking clubs who meet every morning at the local shopping mall. They use the mall to exercise, not to shop. They have no intention of shopping. Once their walk is over, they jump in their car and go shop somewhere else!

Likewise, hits on a website are just people going out for a stroll on the Internet. Hits don't bring in revenue. Sales bring in revenue! And the truth is, most e-commerce sites are hurting for sales.

Why? Because at most sites, shoppers have no incentive to make weekly and monthly purchases. Internet users have no loyalty because most e-commerce sites are more concerned about offering the lowest price than they are about building long-term relationships!

Internet's Biggest Problem — little loyalty

Relationships to the Rescue!

What's the secret to creating customer loyalty in the Internet Age?

Relationships.

Establishing real, rock-solid, long-term relationships with real people (as opposed to hi-tech relationships with "eyeballs" and "hits") is what will separate the successful e-commerce sites from the has-beens.

You see, the hi-tech of the Internet needs the hi-touch of person-to-person relationships. As John Naisbitt observed 20 years ago, "The more hi-tech we have, the more hi-touch we need." That's why today, more than ever, people seek out and need the warmth of the human touch to counterbalance the cold environment of dot-coms and digits.

Think for a moment — did you choose the last movie you saw from a website's banner ad? Doubtful. Most likely a friend or co-worker recommended the movie. Same goes for your favorite websites — most likely they were recommended by someone you knew and trusted, as opposed to your falling for a slick TV commercial or clicking on a rotating banner ad.

Truth is, word-of-mouth recommendations have always been the most effective form of advertising. That's especially true today. You see, people like dealing with people. People trust and value hi-touch relationships. Don't you? And relationships solve the Internet's biggest problem — a lack of loyal customers.

That's where you come in.

You recommend products and services all day, every day, for free. And people shop and buy based on your recommendations. Wouldn't it be great to get paid for it?

You can!

By leveraging your time and relationships, you can create loyal customers for relationship-driven e-commerce sites... while creating a pipeline of ongoing residual income for yourself!

It's a win/win. The e-commerce site gets more loyal customers. And you get paid for recommending products and services you use and enjoy.

I call it the Ultimate Pipeline.

And it's just waiting to be tapped... BY YOU!

Ultimate Pipeline

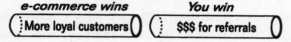

e-commerce wins   *You win*

More loyal customers $$$ for referrals

You Talk... They Tech

Basically, here's how the Ultimate Pipeline works: You and an established e-business enter into an affiliate partnership.

Your role is to "talk" — you direct people to the company's e-commerce site. In return for your recommendations, the e-biz pays you a commission on all the products purchased by your referrals.

The e-commerce company's role is to "tech"

— they provide the website... take the online orders... ship the products... process the credit cards... and handle the accounting. In return for paying out referral fees, the company gets loyal customers who return to the site again and again.

As I said, it's a win/win! The company solves its biggest problem — lack of loyal customers. And you build a pipeline of ongoing residual income.

You talk. They tech. It's simple — brilliantly simple!

With the Ultimate Pipeline, you don't need any special skills. You do what you do every day — you talk to people! You help people cut through the clutter of the Internet... and you get paid for it!

How much can you earn from your Ultimate Pipeline? That's up to you. The sky's the limit! The more people in your referral network, the bigger your residual pipeline. In fact, it's not uncommon for people to receive residual income from tens of thousands of referrals... even hundreds of thousands of referrals!

How could one individual personally recommend products to tens of thousands of people? "That's impossible!" you may say.

Not if you use the magic of compounding! As you will soon see, Einstein had good reason to call compounding "the eighth wonder of the world."

e-Compounding: The Ultimate Pipeline

Do you remember the earlier story about the

Chinese emperor and the inventor of chess?
The inventor only wanted one grain of rice for
his compensation, but he wanted it doubled for
each square on the chess board. The total ended
up being 10 times more rice than there was in
the entire world! The story illustrates the amazing power of compounding, also known as the
doubling concept.

Just imagine for a moment what would happen if you took the concept of compounding...
and somehow combined it with e-commerce.
The result would be "e-compounding."

Power of Compounding

°	:	::	8	16	32	64	128
256	512	1K	2K	4K	8K	16K	32K
....	....	....	....	....	....	....	....
....	....	....	....	....	....	....	....
....	....	....	....	....	....	....	....

Just think of the potential of e-compounding — the exponential growth of compounding... combined with the reach and speed of the
Internet. WOW!

Well, that's why I call e-compounding the Ultimate Pipeline — you get paid to compound
your time and relationships via the Internet!
Just think, with e-compounding, you can get the
results of the Palm Beach Pipeline without having to invest a fortune.

Instead of leveraging your money, you leverage your time and relationships to build your own Ultimate Pipeline! Now it's time to find out how:

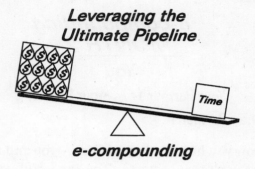

Leveraging the Ultimate Pipeline

e-compounding

e-Compounding Math: (1 + 1) x 12 = BOOM!

Do you think it's possible to find just one person each month to join you in your new e-compounding business? Just one partner who's interested in more financial security... more freedom... more recognition... and more happiness? ... One good person a month — that's all it takes.

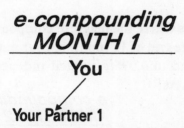

e-compounding MONTH 1
You

Your Partner 1

Once you partner with that new person, you become his or her coach You teach him how to form affiliate partnerships with his friends and acquaintances, while you partner with a second person. So, by the end of month two, you would have two affiliate partners; meanwhile, your first partner has also brought a new person into your affiliate network.

e-compounding ### MONTH 2

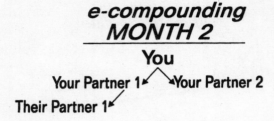

Now you have a group of four — you and three others, isn't that correct? (You can build your e-compounding network faster by partnering with more people each month, but let's assume you take the slow and steady course.)

Then you keep repeating the process. By the end of the first year, you would have personally partnered with 12 people — one new person each month. And let's assume that each one of them has partnered with one new person each month, as well.

This is where the magic of compounding kicks in. By the end of 12 months, your network could compound to 4,096 affiliated independent business owners!

e-compounding ### MONTH 12

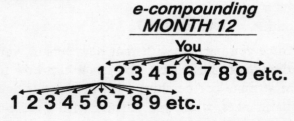

Total: 4,096 people

Now, here's the really exciting part — the e-commerce company pays you a percentage of the sales volume of your entire affiliate network. If you have 4,000 people buying an average of $100 worth of products each month, the total product volume is $400,000 — A MONTH! If your e-biz partner pays you 1% to 3% of that volume, you'd be earning $4,000 to $12,000 a month!

e-compounding

Time & Relationships → Ultimate Pipeline → Residual Income

Now do you see why I call e-compounding the Ultimate Pipeline? It combines the exponential growth of compounding with the convenience and the reach of e-commerce. Not only does the Ultimate Pipeline keep pumping out profits, but, like Pablo, you grow your pipeline by leveraging your time, instead of your money!

No Special Skills Required

The beauty of e-compounding is that you don't need a lot of money to get started. It only takes months or a few years to build, as opposed to decades. And you don't need any special skills. You just do what you do every day — talk to people!

You help people cut through the confusion and clutter of the Internet — and you get paid for it! If you can talk... and point and click... then you can leverage your time and your relationships to build the Ultimate Pipeline.

The Ultimate Pipeline lets us learn from the Palm Beach Pipeline people — we copy the concept of compounding. But instead of compounding our money, we compound our time and relationships. As a result, we can get the results of a Palm Beach Pipeline at a fraction of the money — and in a fraction of the time!

That's why hundreds of thousands of average people all over the world are busy building Ultimate Pipelines — they can enjoy the same benefits the rich enjoy with their Palm Beach Pipelines, but instead of having to leverage a ton of money, they leverage their time! Instead of having to wait 50 years to receive the benefits of their pipeline, they can start enjoying profits in months!

It's a no-brainer!

2 Types of Leverage

Rich People Leverage Money

Average People Leverage Time

Investments   *e-compounding*

New Business Model for a New Millennium

Gary Hamel, author of the bestseller *Leading the Revolution*, says that in a hi-tech world, "Only those companies that are capable of creating industry revolutions will prosper in the New

Economy." Hamel argues that today, companies will compete not in products and services but in the ability to devise ideas for innovative businesses.

He goes on to say that creating better business concepts is nothing new. Henry Ford's breakthrough concept was to make a car that any working man could afford. Ford originally built one car to fit everyone's needs — "You can have any color Model T you want so long as it's black," was Ford's response to requests for more variety.

Alfred Sloan at General Motors improved on Ford's concept. He understood that the customer is king, and he sought ways to meet individual needs and tastes. Sloan's now-famous slogan was "A car for every purpose and purse." Because of Sloan's better business concept, GM vaulted past Ford. Today GM is the biggest revenue-producing company in the world.

New and Improved Model

Like GM, e-compounding is an improvement on the original e-commerce concept, a better way of attracting new customers and fostering their loyalty. E-compounding reminds me of *The Family Circus* cartoon where five-year-old Dolly explains to her younger brother where butterflies come from:

"Butterflies are new and improved caterpillars," she says.

Well, e-compounding is new and improved

e-commerce! Without word-of-mouth marketing... referral fees... and the power of compounding, e-commerce would never have broken out of its cocoon.

e-commerce vs. e-compounding

| Lacks loyal customers | Lots of loyal customers |

But e-compounding offers a new and improved way for e-commerce to sprout its wings and fulfill its potential. As a result, referral-based Internet companies are flourishing while hundreds of deep-discount e-tailers are drowning in debt.

But instead of a car for every purpose and purse, e-compounding is a pipeline for every purpose and purse.

Your purpose may be to earn enough money to afford an extra-nice Christmas. Or your purpose may be to escape from a dead-end job and build Ultimate Pipelines that will circle the globe.

And your purse may be to earn a few extra dollars a month. Or your purse may be to become a millionaire many times over.

E-compounding is the Ultimate Pipeline.

How big you build it is up to you.

Which Ultimate Pipeline Do You Prefer?

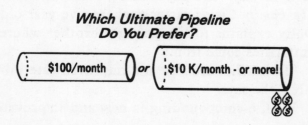

Do You Prefer the 50-Year Plan?... Or the Five-Year Plan?

> Sadly, most bucket carriers would hastily dismiss the notion of a pipeline. Pablo and Bruno heard the same excuses over and over.
>
> It made Pablo and Bruno sad that so many people lacked vision.
>
> — from *The Parable of the Pipeline*

Here's an old joke that teaches two important lessons about pipelines:

A man named Joe worked for years in a low-paying job he hated. But Joe was determined to retire rich. So he scrimped and saved every penny he could and worked nights and weekends in a second job to fuel his investment pipeline.

After 50 years, his discipline and sacrifice paid off. He was finally financially free!

Joe decided that now that he was 70 years old, he was going to live it up! He decided it was time to indulge his life-long dream of scuba diving all over the world. Joe spent thousands of his hard-earned dollars on lessons and diving equipment. He flew first class to Hawaii, where he had reserved a suite at the Ritz Carlton.

The next day he headed out to dive Hawaii's most beautiful reef. His dream had finally come true! He felt a sense of pride as he suited up in his expensive equipment — custom-made wet suit... specially built aluminum oxygen tanks.... German-engineered underwater cameras... water-proof pen and underwater pad for writing notes. Joe was ready!

Joe savored every moment as he swam down toward the rainbow-colored coral reef. He photographed the exotic fish as he descended. His first dive was everything he had dreamed about. He had spent tens of thousands of dollars on his new hobby, but it was worth every penny!

"This was worth the wait," Joe said to himself. "This is perfect!"

Suddenly, Joe was shocked to see a man swimming 10 feet below him wearing only swimming trunks. Joe furiously scribbled a message on his notepad. Then he flippered down to the man and tapped him on the shoulder. Joe scowled as he handed the man the notepad with this message:

"I spent thousands of dollars on scuba diving equipment, and here you are in just your swimming suit. What gives?"

The man grabbed the pad and wrote, *"I'm drowning!"*

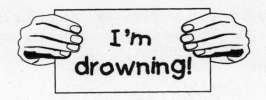

Lots of People Are Drowning

The first lesson we learn from this joke is that things aren't always what they seem! Joe thought the guy was enjoying a leisurely dive. But the truth was much different — the guy was drowning!

Appearances can be deceiving when it comes to finances, too. People who wear Rolex watches and designer clothes appear to be financially independent — but many of them are drowning in debt!

When Thomas J. Stanley and William D. Danko, the authors of *The Millionaire Next Door*, started researching their book, they sought interviews with people who had a net worth of a million dollars or more. Assuming that the richest people lived in the most expensive houses, the authors surveyed people in upscale neighborhoods across the country.

But the authors soon discovered that many people living in big homes and driving expensive cars hadn't accumulated much wealth. Why? Because they were spending their money to support lavish lifestyles instead of putting a portion of it aside to build pipelines.

Stanley and Danko adopted a folksy Texas saying to describe these mega-consumers: "Big Hat, No Cattle." The cowboy metaphor paints a pretty vivid picture, doesn't it?

Big Hat, No Cattle

The Power of the 50-Year Pipeline Plan

The second lesson that we learn from the diving story involves Joe's plan to become financially independent. Joe's 50-year pipeline plan is a classic example of the good news/bad news scenario. Let's look at the good news first.

The good news about the 50-year pipeline plan is that it works! Saving and investing small amounts of money in the stock market on a monthly basis over time is a sure-fire way for people of modest means to become financially independent.

The key to long-term investing is to make regular deposits over a long period of time and then let it compound year after year. If people start early enough and stick to their pipeline plan, they can become millionaires by saving just $100 a month! Impossible, you say? The following chart tells the tale:

How to Accumulate $1 million by Age 65
Assuming a 12% annual interest rate*

Starting Age	Daily Savings	Monthly Savings	Yearly Savings	Years It Takes to Build $1 Million
25	$ 3.57	$ 109	$ 1,304	40 years
35	$ 11.35	$ 345	$ 4,144	30 years
45	$38.02	$1,157	$13,879	20 years
55	$156.12	$4,749	$56,984	10 years

from *The Wise Investor* by Neil E. Elmouchi

* Considering that the stock market has averaged 11% over the last 70 years and 25% over the last decade, 12% is a fair and reasonable rate of return.

It's amazing to learn that it's easy to become a millionaire if you start building your long-term pipeline early enough. Virtually anybody living above the poverty line can do it!

All anyone needs to do is to invest $3.57 a day, every day, in a mutual fund returning 12% interest, and let it compound for 40 years. Instant millionaire! (Well, maybe not "instant" — but definitely a millionaire!)

Think of it this way — one out of three Americans smokes cigarettes. In Florida, a pack of cigarettes costs about $3.57. If every person who smoked quit at age 25 and invested their cigarette money in the market and let it compound for 40 years, one-third of Americans would be millionaires by the time they turned 65!

Isn't that amazing? Don't you wish someone

had pointed that out to you when you were 25 years old? Even at 35 and 45, it's still possible for the average household to build a million-aire pipeline. But people who wait until they're 55 to start saving for retirement are facing a steep mountain, that's for sure!

The Biggest Risk Is NOT Investing in the Market

Many people still think it's too risky to invest in the stock market. And, yes, some stocks go down. And sometimes the entire market goes down, as it did in the crash of 1929.

But all of the wizards on Wall Street say that over time, investing in the stock market is the easiest and surest way to build a profit-pumping pipeline. The facts support the experts: During the 200-plus years the New York Stock Exchange has been in business, stocks have averaged going up two out of every three days. Since WWII, the stock market has gone up 71-fold, despite nine recessions during that 55-year span.

According to Jeremy Siegel's book *Stocks for the Long Run*, in the 195 years from 1802 to 1997, a dollar invested in gold would have grown to just $11.17. That same dollar invested in stocks would have compounded to $7.5 million!!

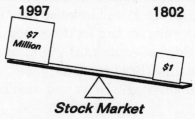

The point is that building a 50-year pipeline has its place, no doubt about it! Most people have several 50-year pipelines under construction. Their home is one long-term pipeline. Social Security is yet another. Unfortunately, all too many people stop at these two pipelines.

Most People's 50-Year Pipeline Plan

ⓢ Social Security
ⓢ Their Home

Smart people, on the other hand, continue to build additional long-term pipelines through investment portfolios... pension plans... IRAs... and the like. All of these are great long-term pipelines, and they're available to anyone with the good sense and the discipline to build them over time.

Smart People's 50-Year Pipeline Plan

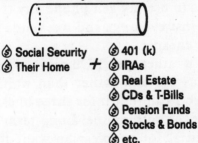

ⓢ Social Security   ⓢ 401 (k)
ⓢ Their Home   **+**   ⓢ IRAs
                    ⓢ Real Estate
                    ⓢ CDs & T-Bills
                    ⓢ Pension Funds
                    ⓢ Stocks & Bonds
                    ⓢ etc.

Downside to the 50-Year Plan

Okay, I just told you the good news about the

50-year pipeline plan — virtually every working family can build a million-dollar pipeline if they start saving monthly and allowing their investments to compound over time.

But the bad news is that most people want to enjoy the benefits of a pipeline today — instead of having to wait 20... 30... 40... or even 50 years!

I admit it — I want to enjoy the finer things in life today, not half a century down the road! Yes, I believe in building long-term pipelines. I have several under construction. But the truth is, I'd rather spend money than save it. I like the things money can buy. I expect you feel the same way, too.

I enjoy a great meal in a first-class restaurant.

I like taking my family on ski vacations and cruises — we've created some of our best memories during vacations.

I love the smell of new car interiors.

I like driving a big Mercedes more than a small Mazda.

I want to use my cell phone any time of the day, not just evenings and weekends when the rates are cheaper.

And I'd rather spend $20 going to a hit movie as soon as it's out, rather than waiting three months so I can rent it for three bucks.

Here's the bottom line: Long-term pipelines are essential for people who want to enjoy a worry-free retirement. That's why everyone should build 50-year pipelines.

But let's get real — do you really want to wait

50 years to enjoy the benefits of a pipeline? Not me! I'm willing to make sacrifices to build my retirement pipeline. But I don't want to have to live like a monk for 50 years in order to do it!

I want to live my dreams right now, while I'm still young and the kids are at home. I don't want to wait until I'm 65 or 70 to start living my dreams — like the scuba diver in the opening story. I'm sure you feel the same.

Have Your Cake and Eat It, Too!

As I said earlier, a long-term pipeline should be at least one of the pipelines you build. But not the only pipeline you build. Just as you shouldn't put all your eggs in one basket, you shouldn't put all your profits in one pipeline.

Well, with the 5-year pipeline plan, you can not only diversify your portfolio of pipelines, but you can dream big dreams and start living them right away, instead of when you're in your 60s or 70s. You can have your cake and eat it, too!

Think about it — wouldn't you rather be financially free in five years instead of 50 years? Of course you would. Who wouldn't?

That's why I recommend you build your 5-year pipeline while you're building your 50-year pipelines!

2 Types of Pipelines

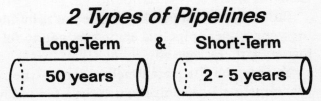

Long-Term & Short-Term

50 years   2 - 5 years

The Ultimate Pipeline — e-compounding—
can be built in two to five years, instead of 50...
and it can start pumping profits within months
instead of decades. You can start building your
Ultimate Pipeline part-time, in the evenings and
weekends, until gradually, it pumps enough
profits for you to begin building it full time!

Just think — the Ultimate Pipeline can get
you to the top of the oak tree in a fraction of the
time that it would take a 50-year pipeline. And
best of all, you don't have to save or invest a
truck-load of money to build your 5-year Pipeline! All you need to do is leverage your time
and your relationships!

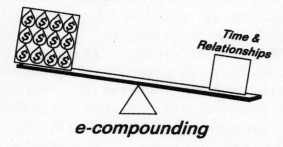

e-compounding

Live for Today... Plan for Tomorrow

Years ago my father gave me some great advice.
He said, "Live for today, plan for tomorrow."
I've never forgotten those words, and I repeat
them regularly to my four children.

Building a 5-year pipeline while you're building your 50-year pipeline empowers you to follow my father's sage advice.

You see, the Ultimate Pipeline plan — the 5-
year pipeline — enables you to live for today

because you can start enjoying the fruits of your labor within months! The 50-year pipeline plan, on the other hand, allows you to plan for tomorrow. That's why I advise people to build both long-term and short-term pipelines!

Pipelines Are Your Lifelines

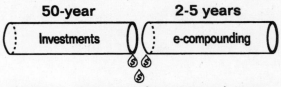

When my father advised me to "Live for to-day, plan for tomorrow," what he was really saying was "Pipelines are your lifelines. So become a pipeline builder, not a bucket carrier."

Great advice, Dad. Great advice.

CONCLUSION:

CONCLUSION

The Parable of the Ultimate Pipeline

Year 2001, Silicon Valley, USA

ONCE UPON A TIME VERY, VERY RE-CENTLY, two ambitious young cousins named Paul and Bruce worked side by side as middle managers for Cistern International, a multi-national conglomerate that owned electric and water utilities all over the world.

The young men were best buddies.

And big dreamers.

They would talk about how some day, some way, they would become totally financially free. They were both bright and hard working. All they needed was an opportunity.

One day that opportunity arrived. The company decided to appoint the two friends as senior managers in Cistern's worldwide software division. Their monthly salary was double what it had been.

"This is our dream come true!" shouted Bruce. "I can't believe our good fortune."

But Paul wasn't so sure.

At the end of the first 10-hour day, Paul's back ached and his finger tips were sore from customizing software. He was in charge of 50 employees, most of whom were uncooperative and unmotivated. He loathed the idea of traveling to foreign offices for weeks at a time. His boss at Cistern was moody, rude, and demanding. Paul dreaded getting up and going into work the next morning. He vowed to think of a better way of living and working.

Paul, the Pipeline Man

"Bruce, I have a plan," Paul said the next morning before they settled into their cubicles and booted up their servers.

"Instead of trading our time and talents answering to a tyrant of a boss and managing unmotivated employees in exchange for a weekly paycheck, let's leverage the Internet to create residual income.

"Having a job is like carrying buckets," Paul continued. "One bucket of work equals one bucket of pay. But if the work stops because of illness or layoffs, the paychecks stop."

A Job

1 Bucket Work = 1 Bucket Pay

"We need a career that will create ongoing residual income. Residual income is like building a pipeline — we do the work once and get paid over and over again. Bruce, we need to start thinking and acting like pipeline builders instead of bucket carriers.

Pipeline

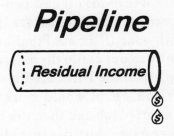

"A former employee of mine is helping me build a pipeline on the Internet. He calls it the Ultimate Pipeline because it combines the power of e-commerce with the power of compounding. The Ultimate Pipeline is my business — I own it. I work from home. There's no overhead. No employees. No payroll. No inventory to speak of. It's lean. It's mean. It's Web-based. And it offers a way to create ongoing residual income."

Ultimate Pipeline

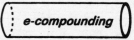

* No boss
* Security
* Freedom
* Independent
  business owner

* No employees
* No payroll
* Small inventory
* No overhead

Bruce stopped dead in his tracks.

"A pipeline on the Internet! Whoever heard of such a thing!" Bruce shouted.

"We've got a great job," Bruce said emphatically. "Don't rock the boat! We've got job security with great benefits.

"We have weekends off and two-weeks' paid vacation every year. We're set for life! Get out of here with your Ultimate Pipeline!"

But Paul was not easily discouraged. He patiently explained the Ultimate Pipeline plan to his best friend. Paul would work part of the day at his salaried job and then use his evenings and weekends to build a pipeline on the Internet.

Paul also knew it would take a year, possibly two, before his Ultimate Pipeline would be big enough to start pumping big profits. But Paul believed in his dream of owning his own business... and owning his own life. He was determined to make it work.

Small Actions Equal Big Results

While Bruce sat in his La-Z-Boy recliner on evenings and weekends, Paul kept building his Ultimate Pipeline.

The first few months Paul didn't have much to show for his efforts. The web-based pipeline business was new to him. He had to learn a new system and teach it to others. He talked daily to his mentors and attended weekend trainings to improve his business-building skills. He read personal growth books and listened to tapes recommended by his mentors.

Day by day, Paul improved his business-building skills. He learned how to engage people in conversations. How to get people to talk about their dreams. How to handle objections gracefully. How to coach people to bring out the best in them. Gradually, he began to believe more and more in himself... in his opportunity... and in his new business partners. This was new territory for Paul. But as his knowledge and confidence grew, so did his Internet pipeline.

Paul kept reminding himself that tomorrow's dreams are built on today's sacrifices. Day by day he built his Ultimate Pipeline, one conversation at a time.

"If my dream is big enough, the facts don't count," he chanted to himself as he picked up the phone to call another prospect.

"Short-term investment equals long-term rewards," he reminded himself as he set his daily and weekly goals, knowing that, over time, the results would far exceed the effort.

"Keep your eyes on the prize," he repeated over

and over as he drifted off to sleep while listening to a training audio by a successful e-biz builder.

"Keep your eyes on the prize...."

The Tables Are Turned

Days turned into months.

One day Paul realized that his e-pipeline was pumping enough profits to equal half his monthly salary! Paul continued to work hard at his day job, but he used his spare time even more productively. He knew it was only a matter of months before his part-time pipeline income exceeded the income from his full-time job.

During his lunch breaks at Cistern, Paul would watch his old friend Bruce scurrying from cubicle to cubicle. Bruce's bucket-carrying job was beginning to take its toll. Bruce was looking more and more stressed by a demanding boss... unrealistic deadlines... and daily rumors of layoffs.

On weekends, Bruce would write dozens of resignation letters. But he never mailed them. He had bills to pay. He needed his paycheck too much to quit. He felt trapped. He felt empty inside. The waste basket in his office wasn't empty, however. It was filled to the brim with wadded up resignation letters....

Resigning from His Job

Finally, Paul's big day arrived — his monthly

e-pipeline check exceeded his monthly salary at Cistern! His wife made color copies of his check from Cistern and the check from his new e-business and framed them side by side. His new pipeline partners cheered as he held up the framed checks. Cameras flashed. And Paul's eyes glistened with joy.

One Day in the Future

Pipeline Income　　　Job Income

Paul was the only worker at Cistern who wasn't intimidated by his boss. Because of his Ultimate Pipeline, Paul was free! That knowledge gave Paul confidence. Paul handled his boss's outbursts calmly. Paul squared his shoulders and looked right in his boss's eye during his tirades.

"It's not necessary to shout," Paul would say firmly. "I'm standing right here in front of you. Wouldn't you agree we'd be more effective if we discussed this calmly?"

Paul's co-workers began calling him the Lion Tamer for he way he handled his boss. But Paul understood that he wasn't taming his boss. Paul was only standing up to him because he no longer had the power to control Paul's life.

One evening Paul sat down in his home-based office and wrote the following letter:

Dear Mr. Boss:

I am writing to inform you that effective immediately, I am resigning from Cistern International.

 I have enjoyed my time at Cistern, but I regret to inform you that the company can no longer afford my services.

Yours Freely,
"Pipeline Paul"

Paul felt a surge of freedom as he folded his resignation letter and inserted it into an envelope. He looked forward to the future with hope and optimism. Paul understood that what he'd accomplished with his Internet pipeline was only the first stage of a big, big dream.

You see, Paul had plans that reached far beyond the walls of Cistern Industries.

Paul planned to build Internet pipelines all over North America — and eventually, all over the world!

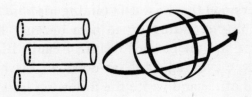

Recruiting His Friend to Help

Paul's web-based business continued to flourish. He had never been happier... or more fulfilled. But the same couldn't be said for his former co-workers at Cistern. The company was moving more and more of their business online, which meant Paul's old department was downsized.

Because of his big salary, Bruce was the first to go. It pained Paul to see Bruce begging his friends for consulting work on their outdated PCs. So Paul arranged a meeting with Bruce.

"Bruce, I've come to ask for your help."

Bruce straightened his stooped shoulders, and his dark eyes narrowed to a squint.

"Don't mock me," Bruce hissed.

"I haven't come to gloat," said Paul. "I've come to offer you a great business opportunity. It took me two years before my Internet pipeline was pumping enough profits for me to resign from Cistern. But I've learned a lot since then. I know how to build Ultimate Pipelines. How to talk to people. How to build teams. How to grow a business by growing people. I've learned a proven system that will empower me and my partners to build another Ultimate Pipeline... and then another... and another.

Pipeline Building System

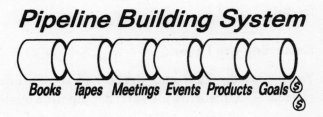

Books Tapes Meetings Events Products Goals

"I need pipeline partners," Paul continued. "I'll teach you everything I know about building web-based pipelines... and I won't charge you one red cent for it. All I ask in return is that you learn the system I teach you and then teach it to others... and have each of them teach it to others... until there are Ultimate Pipelines in every city in North America... and eventually, Ultimate Pipelines in every household in every city in the world.

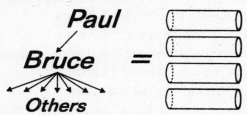

"Just think," Paul continued. "We could make a small percentage of every online purchase that goes through our Ultimate Pipelines. The more volume that goes through our online pipelines, the more money that will flow into our pockets. The Ultimate Pipeline I built isn't the end of a dream. It's only the beginning!"

Paul finally saw the Big Picture. He smiled and extended his hand to his cousin. They shook hands... and then hugged like long-lost friends.

Returning the Favor

Years passed. Paul and Bruce had long since retired. Their worldwide Internet pipeline businesses were still pumping millions of dollars a year into their bank accounts.

The old friends had time to travel and visit exotic places all over the world. One day, Bruce asked Paul to meet him for lunch. He had some exciting news to share.

"Paul, years ago you gave me a very special gift by sharing a web-based business opportunity with me. That gift changed my life forever. I've been racking my brain for years trying to think of a way to repay the favor. That's why I invited you here today. Here's my gift to you."

Bruce slid an envelope toward Paul. Inside were two first-class tickets to Italy.

2 Tickets to Italy

"You don't have to...," Paul started. But Bruce cut his friend short.

"Let me do the talking for right now," said Bruce. "Ever since we were little kids, our parents have been telling us that our families emigrated from Italy. Well, with the help of the Internet, I've been able to trace our family roots back to two cousins who lived in a small village in central Italy.

"Paul, this is my gift to you," Bruce continued. "We're going to return to that village.

We're going to walk to the town square where our great-great-great-great grandfathers and all of the other villagers met to fill their buckets from the town cistern. And we're going to get down on our knees and thank our forefathers and God for building a pipeline of blessings that has flowed freely into our lives."

Coming Full Circle

Paul stared at his cousin in stunned silence. Then he reached over and held both of Bruce's hands firmly in his. "I only have one request," Paul said quietly. "Can you change the departure date from next week to tomorrow?"

# # #

Two weeks later....

The airport in Rome was packed. Paul and Bruce were returning to the states after two wonderful weeks in Italy. They'd walked the streets of their forefathers. And dined in the homes of dozens of long-lost relatives.

It was the trip of a lifetime, and both men felt renewed and reconnected by the visit. They sat side by side in the terminal, reading copies of the same book. Every now and then one of the men would lean over to his friend and point out a passage from the book.

"Uh-h-h-h, NO! — not again" cried a man across the aisle. *"My flight has been canceled —*

AGAIN! I'll never get out of here!"

"That's our flight, too," said Paul motioning to the monitor suspended above them. "Canceled. Now what?"

Paul looked over to his old friend. Bruce returned the look — and then they just smiled.

"You thinking what I'm thinking?" asked Bruce with a smile.

"You thinking what I'm thinking?" grinned Paul.

"Looks like we've got to stay another week!" they shouted in unison as they jumped out of their seats to high five each other.

The man across the aisle gawked at the two friends as if they were aliens.

"What are you guys so happy about?" he asked incredulously. "I've been stuck in this airport for two days. I missed my daughter's birthday party for the second year in a row. I've been in so many time zones during the past month that I don't know what day it is. If that's not enough, I'm going to miss my numbers for the year because my client got greedy and refused to settle."

"We're sorry," said Bruce. "We can sympathize. We used to react the same way, didn't we Paul?"

"Sure did," said Paul. "Stressed out. Tapped out. Burned out. Worn out. You think of an 'out,' and we had experienced it. That was way back in the pre-pipeline days, right Bruce?"

"What do you mean, 'pre-pipeline days?'" asked the stressed out stranger. "What's that all about?"

"Love to explain," Paul said happily. "But my friend and I have to scoot over to the car rental desk. Give me your business card, and one of us will call you when we get back to the states."

The stressed stranger handed Paul his business card. In exchange, Paul handed him his book.

"Here, read this while you're waiting for your flight," Paul said. "When I call you, the book will give us something to talk about."

Paul patted Bruce on the back and steered him toward the rental car desk. He paused long enough to read the stressed stranger's business card.

Bob Bruno, Esq.
ATTORNEY AT LAW

1-800-SUE-THEM

"Bob Bruno, Attorney At Law," Paul said. "I'd say Mr. Bruno would welcome the opportunity to build a pipeline, wouldn't you?"

"Bruno. Bruno." Bruce slowly pronounced the name. "The name Bruno sounds awfully familiar."

"For some reason, Bruce, I've got a good feeling about this guy Bruno," Paul said. "Same feeling I had when you joined me in the business. I think our new friend Bruno is going to be one fine pipeline builder!"

Paul and Bruce glanced back at their new acquaintance.

The stressed-out attorney cradled the book in his lap. Staring intently at the cover, he mouthed the title silently to himself.

Then, gently, like an old man opening a gift from his favorite grandchild, Bruno opened the book called *The Parable of the Pipeline* — and he began to read....